The Hidden Ancestral Identity of the American "Negro"

RaDine America Harrison

Hidden Ancestral identity of the American Negro
America, RaDine, 1957-

Copyright © 2001 Quantum Leap S.L.C. Publications

Published in America by Quantum Leap S.L.C. Publications.

Cataloging-in-Publication Data
America, RaDine, 1957-
The Black American Handbook For Survival Through the 21st Century –
Volume I   -- 1st ed.
p. cm.
Includes Ind

ISBN 978- 0-9705455-1-0

1. America-Discovery and Exploration   2. Blacks-America-History

3. Indians-Culture.

(Ankh & Feather) Hidden Heritage" Logo Design: Eleyé Eifé, © 1999,
2000Author's Photograph (back page) by: John ZiegleEdited by: Steven P.
Young   Printed in Washita
First Edition: May 2001, Second Edition October 2015
 The Black American Handbook for Survival Through the 21st Century –
Series
The Hidden Ancestral Identity of the American Negro
Also available on Audio Cassette, and Ebook.

For more information or to order copies of this book, contact:
Quantum Leap SLC Publications
P. O. Box 527
Princeton, West Virginia 24740
1-877-571-9788 or 304-212-2362

ISBN:978-0-970545510

Special Thanks

To all the contributions, pictures, technical, support received in the development of the Hidden Ancestral Legacy belonging to today's

"black America"

May our consciousness evolve above the artificial narratives for perceptions that ultimately persecute us. To my kinfolk may we never forget our truth.

In Loving Memory of elder Cecelia E. Bailey

1944-2015

Researcher/Grand Elder

Author's Note: True Freedom and Harmony among all human races of people on Earth <u>can only be attained from facing the truth</u> with <u>all</u> races taking responsibility for their collective actions and effects towards their destruction on Earth..

The Hidden Ancestral Identity of the American Negro is the introduction to a series of books for the People's of America aka black to learn the omitted facts about their historical heritage. The books are intended to give a balanced overview of the true dynamics that is the core foundation for the United States and its relation to the destiny of the Amerindians/ Negro People of the America's called black Americans today.

All books published by Quantum Leap SLC. Publications are written in a format that will give the reader a lot of hidden pertinent facts about their ancestral heritage and history quickly. The information contained in these pages will allow Amerindians as black "America" to identify distorted historical information. and why this distortion exists. In order for the survival of the population of "America" people , the who, what, when, where and why must be identified; and How the methods are being used to create the deep seated sense of powerlessness we are experiencing as a collective today.

First, understanding who you are ,and what you represent must be addressed in order to make the necessary changes in perceptional consciousness that will allow the survival of the OUR people and our future generations in the rapidly changing landscape within America ,the United States, and throughout the new Geo-political world.......

TABLE OF CONTENTS

Preface

Today, most elders over 70 years old in black "America" will   tell you that they are not descendants from stolen people from Africa ,who came to America on boats as slaves or sharecroppers, nor do they consider themselves as having a blood(DNA)heritage (mother)connection to Africa as ethically African, They state they are descendants from Indian and Negro grandmothers or they have Indian Blood connection.

If you ask people who are immigrants from the continent of Africa Most people form Africa will admit to the fact that the black people of America ,their Negro ANCESTORS are not RELATED TO THEM AS MIS-PLACED RELATIVES FROM AFRICA LIVING IN AMERICA.

The looming question to be asked is:?

Why is the political narrative of " history" in the United States by institutionalized higher and public education, professional elite, politicians, and US media constantly promoting the only historical narrative for the race of people labelled as black America in the United States is slavery and their   heritage ancestry is captured immigrants from West Africa, as the reason to change their generational political identity with the United States of Negro to a new political identity of African Americans. While completely ignoring their Mothers/grandmothers heritage identity connection to   American "INDIAN" or Amerindian as their ethnic heritage identity behind the label of Negro, as the ancestral origin of today's population of black America ?

The purpose of this book is to clarify the "heritage identity" behind the term "Negro" and help the current remaining generations of population identified as black America to start a honest dialogue with our current elders identified as Negro, *to help clarify why they say they came from grandmothers with American Indian blood, aka Amerindians and remove any conflict and confusion black America have today about the ancestral origins of the blood of their mothers that created them and their roots to a home on Earth before it is to late...

Over the last 110 years or more, institutionalized public education in Early American "His – story" has omitted the facts about the classification for racial identity cloaked behind the colonial identities applied to the female population and their children in the United States classified as Negro...

Who qualifies for this classification? Why is it only given to persons born from light to dark brown skinned females automatically at birth, before ones moral, intelligence or character can be determined to have the prejudices presumed by the classification Negro, aka Nigga (female) or Nigger (male).

Answers to these questions will clarify the connection of the Negro classified population of people in the United States and their direct relationship to the indigenous heritage for "America "race population of the western hemisphere referred to as the vanished race population of the Anisazi Peoples and their cultural civilization identified as the Mound builders.

The intention of this book is to answer these questions with pertinent facts about the foundation behind the colonial racial identity of Negro an its connection to the Original people of "America" colonially labeled at first Indians. Why recognizing the connection between the Indian and Negro is important for the current generations of black America ability to live within the United States in America, and have the ability see what is really happening to them and WHY?.

The book will reveal how the relationship for the/agenda of the Europeans towards claiming the Home on Earth belonging to the heritage of America's Indians aka Amerindians is the narrative towards the constant and deliberate mis-leading perceptions of the American Indians in Early American History, and how these deliberately mis-leading perceptions maintain the foundation for institutionalized and systematic racism towards aka Negro / black "America" by the United States today.

This book will answer, Why the actual events in early American history have been omitted by the U.S. and replaced with an completely artificial narrative for the northern section of the western hemisphere known as North America. The public education historical narrative in the United States about original America is :

,America was/ only inhabited with Asiatic Migrants from Asia following the route of the buffalo living in the southwestern dessert as Indians and all dark skinned /curly to wavy haired people in America are immigrants ,brought to America as imported slaves presumed to be from Africa- called Negros:. This de-humanizing narrative created for the brown skin/curly haired heritage people labeled Negro is one of the many pieces supporting the foundation for today's black "America" distorted perceptions about themselves and their connection to ethnic racial characteristics for their America Indian aka Amerindian grandmothers and their home with their planet Earth origins of their Negro ancestry . This perception to say the least, is shrouded in racism and is a seriously inaccurate one.

"History is a Weapon"

Today, most people in black "America "can identify one or both parents with American Indian grandmothers as ancestors, while ,the majority of the population cannot make a reference from their family members oral heritage about any connection to boats or Africa, however, the population of black America are being influenced to disrespect, discredit and ignore their actual oral heritage intellegence from their oldest living relative to American Indian ancestral heritage identification for their blood connection to the planet Earth ,and adopt idealistic beliefs created by the same foreigners semantic science used to oppress and destroy them. The confusion around the validity of their families oral reference to the American Indian blood origins from whence they came is based on the conditioned perceptions of misrepresentations of racial characteristics of what American Indians as a population looks like, to how the original population of people living in the western hemisphere of North America perceive themselves on their blood soil.

This racial deception about the representation of the Original American people is so deeply rooted in the United States' past that the truth is repeatedly ignored in favor of the romanticized ,idealistic and dehumaninizing narrative perpetuated by Media, educational institutions, and used in governmental policy towards the people of black America. The deliberate AMNESIA BY THE UNITED STATES TO THE FACT THAT THE RACIAL IDENTITY OF ALL People born from females classified as NEGRO/ aka black ARE THE CHILDREN OF AMERICA- the TRUE INDIANS/ INHERITORS by blood TO THE SOIL OF AMERICA. AS WELL AS THE HERITAGE PEOPLE BEING SOCIALLY AND CULTURALLY ENSLAVED (living under occupation) for extermination of them for THEIR SOIL; HAS FAR REACHING EFFECTS.

The result of this amnesia and deception about the Negro people in United States historical record has created an CONFUSION OF IDENTITY (IDENTITY CRISIS) WITHIN the interllectual Consciousness of today's younger generations black "AMERICA", resulting in a DISTORTED ROMANTICISM of BELONGING to WEST AFRICA as their intellectual connection to a place of Earthly belonging and as a way to escape from the demoralizing oppression they experience living under the identity label of Negro or black within the United States...

In return, the real heritage, culture, and home with Earth for TODAY'S generations of black "America" remains invisible. Furthermore, the omission and cover-up of Americas heritage has left all people, who have adopted America as their New homeland, with a FALSE/ artificial narrative to the right of belonging.

The omission of ancestral identity of the Negro, from Early American history in public education has robbed generations of people belonging to America as Negro/ black of a rich cultural heritage, proud ancestral past, inheritance to an home with Earth; and with no true and complete sense of self. . As a result, the young generations of black "America" are LOST, aimlessly living their lives without purpose or direction, they have become an invisible stranger in her and his own home with Earth and is trapped within the FALSE perversions for their racial ethnic identity as being descendants from deported "SLAVES" to America according to colonial " history" and propaganda..

The Africans have a saying,

"If you don't know and respect your heritage (who you are), any history will do."

"WELCOME TO AMERICA."

This is the section on Earth where genocide was and is STILL being committed against populations of indigenous people for their Earth. The fact that most of America today no longer recognize or respect themselves for their Life heritage inheritance from their mothers as the "Children of America "- inheritors to the soil of "America "as their home with Earth is at the core of their ignorance.

Hopefully, our books will start and help to clear the confusion with facts about the true identity of today's black American people and give a strong foundation for understanding the reason behind discrimination, institutionalize racism and the systematic destruction against families and communities of America by the United States . After reading the Hidden Ancestral Identity of the American

Negro, the reader will start to have a better understanding with a new sense of clarity to make corrective actions in their perceptions towards giving positive collective and self-respect for their human ancestral blood heritage origins that is stolen from their mothers belonging to the identity of Negro and to stop supporting their victimization from destructive perceptions that continue to emotionally fuel our/their collective self-destruction

We don't have to be constant Victims.

A People who have no heritage

worth mentioning

are likely to believe

that they have no humanity

worth defending.

They are forever...

...LOST!"

William Katz / Black Indians

Chapter 1

Her-it-age

What is Her-it-age? Her –life- thru time

Heritage of Life is the collective activities used to serve our function as a part of the **nature or eco- system environment** of the planet Earth in our daily living. Heritage is the collective Earth nature that is implemented by **FEMALES of the Earth as Mothers with the Earth to their section of Earth.** This bond between the planet Earth and Earth females or hue-females create the emotional fabric of a race. The fabric that is created by females as mothers over the ages SUPPORTS the balance with the Earths internal SYMBIOTIC emotional MOVEMENT existing WITHIN ALL LIFE FORMS with their collective purpose to Earth.

Life Heritage contains the knowledge needed about how we thrive in our existence as a part of the Nature of Earth, called human nature, and the understanding of why the gift of life with Earth should be respected and given the greatest value.. The results from this knowledge unites, strengthens and maintains our life force connection and function to the Nature of life with our soil inheritance from Earth... Which allows us to experience-

THE JOY OF LIFE LIVING WITH EARTH...

Why is Life Heritage knowledge Important?

The Life Heritage knowledge represents the collective ancestral knowledge about the nature with in us from our Mothers that connects us to where we belong with Earth to continue our collective Life, and the foundational collective purpose as life with Earth. The culture created from our heritage maintains the collective abilities for strength to perform the purpose as life over generation's with Earth. Life Heritage knowledge creates the sense of emotional wellbeing for belonging to the group and the connection to their environment for life living with Earth, The Life heritage knowledge contains acts for the process of Caring or Nurturing life for ourselves and our natural environment These acts of bonding unite the family, community and environment as a part of the whole life support system for Earth.

Life Heritage knowledge is the foundation for the culture, which creates the customs, language, religions, practices, beliefs and the unique charterstics that give collective individuality (identity) and purpose of the heritage people and validates the purpose for human life in nature.

A person's inheritance to an Life heritage and its culture contains the knowledge for self-reliance with Earth that empowers and gives a sense of security about their position as a species within the essence of Earth.. This knowledge gives a person / group / race the resiliency or power to recognize mistakes and gives understanding about the mistakes of the past which creates the history and weakness in the present. Respecting one's life heritage allows a person _**NOT**_ to be trapped in small mindedness, **narcissism**, and irresponsibility with

2

their life inheritance; that will lead to life exploitation and victimization. Life heritage knowledge can counteract the forces of aggression from enemies/ invaders/ oppression tactics directed towards extinction of the species and destruction of the environment that supports the life viability of the Earth and race.

Collective knowledge from one's Life Heritage can allow one to take cognitive actions to stop the mistakes in action that deny the natural emotional flow which can restore balance and harmony , joy and respect for their inherited birthright to Life from Earth thru their mothers. and ensure for future generations the continuation of their life inheritance from Earth to an soil/ environment for life purpose and support with their planet.

Ignorance / disrespect/ distortion of one's awareness of their Life heritage guarantees confusion/ insecurity and fear about taking responsibility for the person's natural place of belonging with their collective humanity and for their environment. This ignorance or distortion of ancestral Life heritage knowledge effectively disables a population or race ability to make effective choices that will defend themselves, and future generations from domestication, self-destruction leading to collective extinction/death from their section with Earth...

Physical Pain , emotional suffering, mental illness, poverty, and disease leading to death is the signal to our physical nature from the Life of Earth's Consciences that resides within us , letting us know we are out of harmony and balance with our purpose for life of Earth.. We are not listening/ operating from our hearts/ truth/ or Natural Law of Life consciouness. Our perceptions / attitudes towards our lives are wrong, which has denied our emotional natural flow of inner consciousness expression through ourselves.

" America" aka blacks/Negro's for the last 140 years to the present, have willingly assimilated into European domestication for the comfort of living irresponsibly as individual slaves. The consequences as a result to Negro/blacks of America, they are systematically disenfranchised and disconnected from the roots (heritage of their blood) which builds/ supports their inner conscious and / personal mental stability for the race population and our future generations... The Negro people aka black "America" still seek to escape taking responsibility for their life purpose by all means possible as a way to run from the disillusionment and frustration from the emotional weakness ,creating fear and insecurity within.

The challenges we all see confronting us is a warning to change and raise our consciousness, look beyond the illusion of the physical/mind(ego) , it is time to find the truth, learn the knowledge of their heritage and follow the ancestral heritage life consciousness that lives in our emotional soul. There is where we will find the solution for the challenge.

All answers for the solution to our peril is inherited in the heart of our essence with our planet Earth. It is time to seriously accept. respect and a pay attention to our heritage , and the principles for life inherited within, then you/we can trust our natural consciousness used to guide our intellect- Return to Natural Law... By learning to Listen and following the emotions of our heart, that lives in our blood. is where the wisdom of your ancestral heritage (Ancestral Grandmother) will be found.

The Hidden Ancestral Identity of the "American Negro"

The Solution to all of our challenges will be found with returning to the allegiance to our Mother of all Life—Earth. This is done by respecting, and taking the time to learn and following the wisdom of our heritage, and uniting with the people who live and can teach the heritage skills. All Black America can attest to the fact that their ancestors' sweat, blood and lives were exploited to build the United States whether under captivity or free..

It is a hidden and ignored fact; the cultural heritage legacy developed in America by the Earth people of "America" over the labyrinth of time with their section of Earth, is the foundation behind the enormous riches claimed by the United States; is stolen from the ancestral heritage cultural civilization created by the Nations of Grandmothers from whence today's black" America" are the current descendants of.

"True comprehension of ones heritage

lends itself to a better grasp

on the present.

It helps us to understand

who we truly are,

and how we came to be

a subjugated people

within this nation today."

Chapter 2

The Hidden Racial Identity of the

Original *People of the Western Hemisphere*

"Understanding "America"

Welcome to America

As you can see the Western Hemisphere of Earth or New World called "America" is represented by a dark skinned female or Negro as your "Highness". If you look closely at the picture, she is standing above a section of Earth globe "America" and her people are not in shackles. The picture clearly depicts male Foreigners / Christians coming from a boat landing on her soil with a cross behind her, to stake a claim to her Earth inheritance including people.

Understanding America

Q. *Who is America?*

A. America is represented by the *indigenous* females for the Western Hemisphere of Earth. *A*merica is represented by dark- skinned females who represent the Human Nature of Earth with the blood connection (DNA) to the soil as heritage of the Females and the males they create to live with this section of Earth. The image of America also represents the Earth expression of females as the *Children of the Forest* or trees..

Q. *What is the original name for the human race of America?*

A. The human race for America identified their collective race tree "Anisazi" people, they are the original people living as the continuation of the population for human species with nature living in their home for

9

Earth in America for thousands of years before discovery by foreigners.

Q; What is the meaning of the term indigenous?

A: Indi-gene-ous; originating or occurring naturally in a particular place; The word Indigenous is an international term to represent the human populations created by the Earth to inhabit a section of Earth.

Indigenous people look like the Environment or soil .

Indigenous blooded people are an integral part of the environmental system to support the life of the planet Earth. They are an internal function for the planet Earth, living as part of the natural environment along with the plants and animals living in the section of Earth.

Indigenous people created by the Earth look like the soil of the Earth. At one time the whole Earth was inhabited by these human populations. The genetics connection to the soil, is in the blood of Earth females and is passed down thru their blood to their new generations of children.. As long as the environment thrives the fertility of the Earth female's ability to cycle their life blood will thrive. When the environment dies, the human nature of females to the soil loses her fertility and starts to die. If the human females and environmental nature is exterminated from the section of Earth SHE is connected to the Earth soil environment   dries up and turns into a dessert.

Q: *Why is the connection to Earth in the human Nature of females blood?*

A: Nature as human females are the physical life creators/portals for emotional consciousness as LIFE on Earth to transform itself into physical form. It is through the   human female's blood', the physical body to hold   /house emotion as life is created.

Males are the pollinators, example- the reproduction with   plants, Males serve the purpose of cross pollination, (by adding additional genetic material for use in the blood) through the process of cross pollination allows the   creation of originality (individuality)   of physical expressions in Life, of the species, for Earth

Q: *Why do all indigenous/ original people have a belonging/home with Earth and birthright given to them by planet Earth to a placement with Earth?*

A: All indigenous people are the Human expression of nature with the Earth, they are the children of the planet Earth. All Earth females carry the genetics in their blood to a connection to the section of Earth they were created to nurture and protect for the Earth. This placement of soil in the Earth is their home with Earth.

It is an unconditional place of belonging, where the environment supports them as they support the environment, a place for our mothers to build Life with Earth upon and to be fruitful and multiply. The traditions and culture developed from nurturing the environment with Earth is where we share our common inheritance by blood of belonging as a part our collective species with our planet Earth.

Q: *What does the term INDIAN mean?*

A: The word **INDIAN** is the European/ English word used to collectively represent the individual to the human nature of a section of Earth as original Earth person. This term was applied to all the **DARK-SKINNED PEOPLE who look like the Soil LIVING in the different sections with the planet Earth** The term was in common use at the time of discovery by Columbus. It was the first term Europeans applied to all dark-skinned people living in North, Central and South America. Example American Indian,

Q: *What geographical areas do the races of people live?*

A: Each **Root race** has a section of the planet Earth.

Picture; look at the statue of America, As you see the statue of Africa and America are dark-skinned peopled..

Africa   Asia   Europe   America

Q: *How many original Earth or Root races are there?*

A: Three: Indo-Asia, Asia Africa and America aka Negro.

Q: *What does the term Negro mean?*

A: The word Negro is a Latin/roman root word used in Spanish, Portuguese, English, French ,German, etc. to represent ancient ones or original humans by blood of the Earth originally applied to the Carthaginian population of Peoples aka Egyptians of North Africa and extended to all populations of people from the Earth heritage living in the western hemisphere as the America's

The term Negro is an international term used to identify the indigenous populations in the western hemispheres born from the females of the human nature to Earth as America. – it also means to foreigners people to attack, enslave, kill and exterminate from their Earth for

13

their Earth inheritance.. Example: Indigenous female of South America in Brazil are identified as Negro/Negras.

Q: *What does the term African mean?*

A: The term African is a roman term used as an semantic term (double meaning) applied to identify persons who are placed under occupation or freedom., aka -collective being stripped of their ability to build/and thrive collectively with their section of Earth. The term is also applied to people who are in the process of being removed from their heritage section of Earth including their human rights , they are considered refugees to the governments occupying the section they currently reside with. The populations the term African is applied to are indigenous people who no longer have/ recognize their heritage right to Earth heritage inheritance as belonging to a section of soil on the planet Earth. African is not an ethnic term. The word represents a condition... In others words used until disposed of...

14

Q: *Which race do today's black America population represent?*

A; The population of black America represents the human root race population for "America" this race inhabited the complete western hemisphere of North, Central and South America, Population race name is " Anisazi".

Other foreign names given to the people of America are: Amerindians American Indians –Negro, Negretos Creoles. Mulattoes , Niggers

Q: *What section of the planet Earth do the Anisazi, aka ,[American Indian/Negro race inhabit?*

A; The complete western hemisphere- Greenland, Canada, North America, Central America, South America, Alaska, Australia, Pacific Islands and the Caribbean Islands.

Q. *What does the word Anisazi mean?*

A. The word Anisazi means "The Ancient One", the Planet Keepers. The people since the beginning of human creation with America

Q: *How many different ethnic groups lived in the western hemisphere before discovery?*

A: Three groups. These groups are:

- The Anisazi- Root race with the largest population living throughout all of the

Americas and their cultural civilization called the Mound/ Pyramid Builders,.

- The South Pacific/Western Plains – Migrant People from Indo- Asia (Asian/ Anisazi mix population)

- The Alaskan (Anisazi , Asian, and Viking mixed population)

Q: *How big was the Human race population in the western hemisphere North America?* *(including central and Caribbean)?*

A: The Anisazi race population was over 500 million-1 billion people.

Q: *What are some of the bloodlines that make up the Nations of North & Southeastern America?*

A: Aniyumwija aka Cherokee, Chickasaw, Muskogees (Creeks), Choctaw, Osage, Algonquin, Delawares, Tuskarora, Riccaree, Mandan, Washitaw, Tunica, Eastern Sioux (Dah-ca-ta), Shawanos, Yamasse, Pawnee, Assininbons, Minatarees, Crows, Comanche, Oneidas, Senecas, Piankeswhaws, Quapaws, Chippeway, Illinois, Sac and Foxes, Ioway, Cheyenne, Apache, Omahas, Ottos Caddo, Konzas, Potawatomies, Pequots, Miamis, Koiwas, Kaskaskias, Mohawks, Mohegans and thousands more...

C H E R O K E E   N A T I O N

When Columbus arrived in America in 1492 the continent was already populated by as many as 40 million people from six hundred or more Native American tribes.

Q: *What do the people who are called the Anasazi or Amerindians of North to SouthAmerica look like?*

A: Descriptions of the Indigenous peoples of America or Anasazi race of the Aniyumwija people (termed Cherokee Nation), Chickasaw, Muskogee ,Choctaw, and many others.

Inquiry into the distinctive characteristics of the Aboriginal Race of America

Boston Society of Natural History 1842

It is chiefly my intention to produce a few of the more strikingly characteristic traits of these people to sustain the position that all American nations, excepting the Eskimaux, are of one race, and that this race is peculiar and distinct from all others.. It is a adage among travelers that he who has seen one tribe of Indians(men) has seen all, so much do the individuals of the race resemble each other, notwithstanding their **immerse** *{***Vast, massive, enormous, gigantic, colossal, great, monumental***} geographical distribution, and those differences of climate which embraces the extremes of heat and cold.*

Physical Characteristics: *All possess alike the long , lank, back hair, the brown or Cinnamon colored skin, the heavy brow, the dull and sleepy eye, the full and compressed lips and the salient but dilated nose.*

.

These , traits, moreover are equally common to the savage and civilized nations; whether they inhabit the margins of rivers and fed on fish, or rove the forest and subsist on the spoils of the chase. It cannot be questioned that physical diversities do occur, equally singular and *inexplicable, as seen in the different shades of color, varying from a fair tint to a complexion almost black; and this too under circumstances in which climate can have little or no influence. In reference to stature, the differences are remarkable in entire tribes, which moreover, are geographically proximate to each other. These facts, however, are mere exceptions to a general rule, and do not alter the peculiar physiognomy [***judging human character from facial features**] of the **Indian;** which is devastatingly characteristic as that of the **Negro**; for whether we see him in the athletic Charib, or the stunted Chayma, in the dark Californian or the fair Borroa, he is an Indian still and cannot be mistaken for being of any other race..*

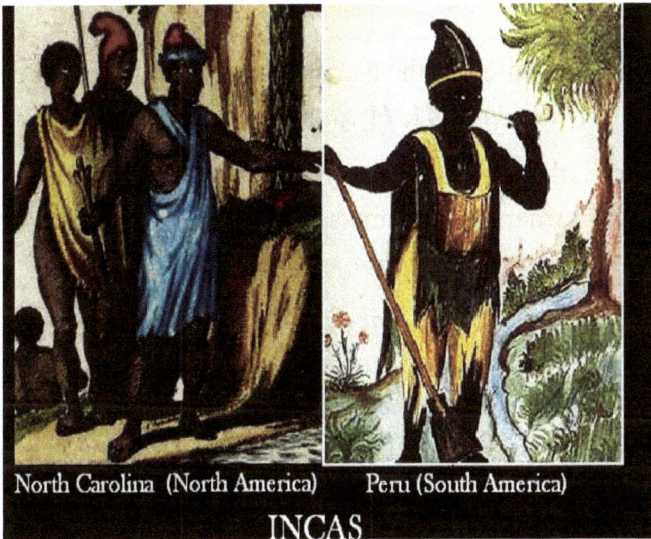

North Carolina (North America)   Peru (South America)
INCAS

The American race contains nations whose features differ as essentially from one another as those of the Circassians, Moors and Persians. But all these people are of one and the same race, and readily recognize as such, not withstanding their differences of features and complexion; and the American nations present a precisely parallel case.

19

Algonquin - Patawomeck People

Letters& Notes on the North American Indians
written in 1841, by author George Catlin.

George Catlin, a noted ethnographer describes indigenous America/ American Indians as: *"All primitive tribes known in America are dark, copper-colored with jet-black hair."* *(Pg.149)*

"Some Amerindians have straight hair while **most possessed curls in the extreme and every level of wavy hair in between.** *Texture of the hair is generally fine, soft as silk or coarse and harsh.*

*" Catlin did not comment that some tribes were dark reddish brown. He stated that **all** Indigenous American people are reddish brown from light to dark.. Simply put, the stereotypical "**White**" female and male as Indians of "America" does not exist.*

20

The truth is race population Indigenous to America or Anisazi are an extremely diverse race of people consisting of reddish brown to deep dark brown people of widely varying types that are the real people of the Americas (North, Central, South and Islands) called America Indians or Negros.

Q: **What kind of hair do the real people Indigenous to North America have?**

A: Today, it's called textured "Kinky" or wavy hair – not straight.

The coarse hair will stand anything and will grow.

The fine hair is delicate and needs a lot of moisture

of the forest to stay silky and grow long.

Catlin also noted, *"The hair of men falling down to the hams and sometimes to the ground, is divided into plaits or slabs two inches width, and filled with a profusion of glue and earth, which becomes very hard and remains unchanged from year to year.* (Today, this form of hair is called "Locks" or "Dread Locks".) Catlin also commented, *"Women used deer oil in their hair and it was long and flowing in plaits or braids. Men wore their hair shaved with a top lock or totally bald."*

Look at the physical features. Do you know someone who resembles them?

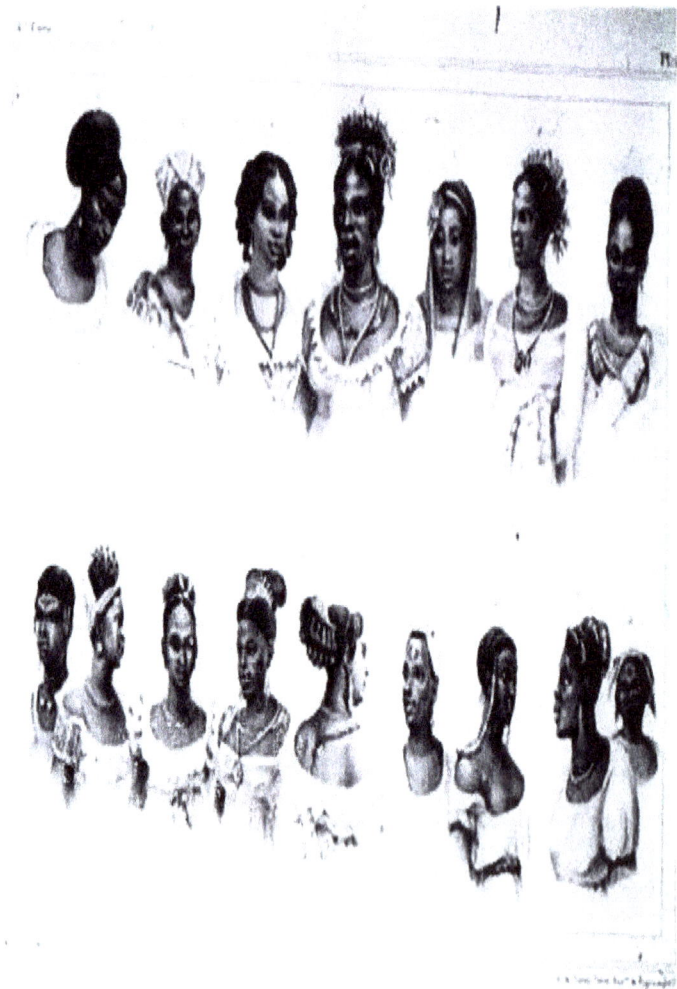

Negros de America

Portrait of captured females from different nations in America, put on display in France, before being used for sex and beaten until the life in them is gone....

Q: *What about the eyes?*

A: Catlin noted, *"Their eyes are black/brown. Eyes can be hazel blue, green, or gray, with mixed complexions from dark brown to very light, as half-breeds."*

And, in the book "Indian America", by Gurko, *"Some have slanted eyes, more   did not, noses are high arched, flared or forehead and nose almost flat."*

For example: look at the features

Q: What about skin color?

A: John Smith, the first English explorer, described the color of the people when he landed on the eastern shore of America, in 1612. Today, this location is called Jamestown, Virginia. He described Powhatan, the Algonquin chief he had encountered to look more *"like a devil than a man, with some two hundred or more men as Black as himself."* *(Our National Archives, Erik Bruun & Jay Crosby)*

23

John Smith continued, *"Some being very large (tall & big) as the Susquehannocks, others very little (short & petite) as the Wighcocomocos; but generally tall and straight, of a comely proportion, and of shades of brown when they are of any age, but they are born white." Example:*

In Chickasaw Nation, by Mason comments, *"Their complexions are of dark reddish- brown or suntan (copper) brown color."*

Q; *What is the physical stature of the Anisazi people of North America?*

A: (Chickasaw Nation, by Mason) comments, "Men are tall, erect and moderately robust, their limbs well shaped, so generally to form the perfect human figure." (*For example:* Michael Jordan.)

"Women of the Cherokee are tall 5' 7" & up, slender   erect delicate frame features with perfect symmetry.   Example:

Muskogee women are very dark-skinned, short in stature, and well formed. Chickasaw women are a good size as well as beautiful. Delaware women are big and rounded or full figured..

Example:

Catlin makes note of all kinds of different sized and shaped people who are part of the many thousands of tribes living on the eastern seaboard and mountains. In some tribes, the men are 7 feet tall with a large stature.

The word **"TRIBE"** means a f<u>amily, community of kinfolk by blood connection..</u>

Q: Are there many SKIN color ranges for Anisazi people as American Indians?

A: Early Spanish explorers noted indigenous America/American Indians were extremely diverse not just in appearance but also in many aspects... Obviously, the people Indigenous to North America are a race of light dark/reddish or brown skinned people as diverse in phenotype (physical) characteristics as any other ethnic group.

25

Look at some of the many skin shades & tones of America.

Q: *Do Anisazi aka American Indians have straight, black hair and tan or white skin?*

A: No. This is a myth, pure and simple; perpetuated today by "Hollywood" and the media, in its many forms. Public education in the United States about the Earth population of America is completely artificial . To keep the children of America accepting foreigners on their life inheritance they are taught to see themselves as foreigners to the United States,, however they are not foreigners to the soil the United States resided on as America. In order to assimilate children of America aka Negro population   for integration into the United States . The United States under President Thomas Jefferson CHANGED the racial and physical characteristics of ***"AMERICA"***

population inheriting America as the   Negro people with an artificial European image to   represent "America' as Columbia. Public education only included the first immigrant population from Asia living in America as belonging to America   before   discovery. Millions of people indigenous to America have been

26

conditioned to   recognize the racial identity and image of their ancestry of   American Indian, as people with long straight Asian hair. Indigenous people to   America hair is naturally bushy like the collective trees tops of the forest. The skin color is the color of the soil ,wood, and the bark of trees.

 Go to the mountains and look at the tops of trees and you will see the reflection of a bushy head like the indigenous hair to America. People indigenous to America skin and hair resembles the red wood trees of the Forest.....

Example: Look at the resemblance of her skin color and the color of the redwood statue.

Look at the Resemblance

Ancestral Past   **Today/   Present**

 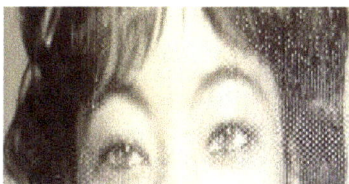

 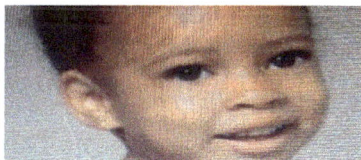

ned head of tattooed man., Palenque
a head with flattened head, Palenque

The past is now present , the blood of the Earth lives in the Children of the planet Earth. "America" is the blood, .All people labeled black Americans today represent the ancestors of the past living in the present. The blood of Earth in America does not LIE. All people born from brown skinned females with above features are labeled Negro's To be labeled Negro means you are the present blood of Earth for America living in America. America's children as Negros . In other words to be an American Indian aka Amerindian is to be a Negro. **American Indian females are not white. The real America is today's black America or Negro females Our wealth is in our Blood..**"

The Blistered Fox, Ioway Medicine Man"
George Catlin

Looks like the late Red Fox. Comedian/ Actor – Sanford and Son. Could this be Redd Fox great, great grandfather?

Look at the last name Fox, Blistered Fox – Redd Fox .

This is a   1822 lithograph of a group of Northern California Indians. Look at the diversity of   features. Today the same people would be regarded as Black Americans

This is a water color by Louis Choris, a artist who visited the Spanish mission called San Fransico with members of a Russian naval expedition in 1822. Look at the features, today these people are called Negro's or black Americans.

Q: *How many years did America the home of the Anisazi people with their civilization called Pyramid/Mound Builders live here?*

A: Artifacts found in Southeastern America are older than the artifacts uncovered in Egypt, they date back as far as 7,000 to 12,000 years.

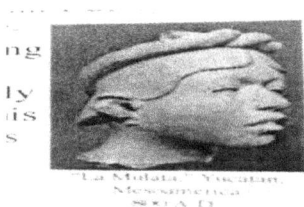

Texexpan woman 11,000 years old new mexicio

Etowah Indians Georgia, USA 1250 AD.

Luzia negroid Brazil 3.2 millions old

Q: *What form of civilization did the human nature of America create?*

A: America lived as an egalitarian hetero sexual culture following their inherited natural Earth consciousness, centered around the human life principles of collective conscience, equality, and oneness with Life for Earth. The uninhibited expression of creativity in Nature thru all living forms. The people of the Earth followed the female as blood descendant not the genetic donor as father. Mother is creator ,Father is pollinator.. Just like in Nature of plants, the female plants house the seed and creation ability ,the male provides the cross pollination as a form of natural defense.

Q: *What does the term Mound Builders refer to ?*

A: The Mound Builders is the colonial name given for the civilization built by the advanced matrilineal egalitarian culture of human nature of the Americas inhabiting the Western Hemisphere or Amerindians. This master race of Earth people built over 250 million earthen-shaped pyramids over the last 12,000 years in the Western Hemisphere over the Eastern portion of North, Central and South America and islands. According to colonial history this vast indigenous matrilineal culture with 400 to 700 million people mysteriously VANISHED from the Western Hemisphere during the 1700's. and was replaced by a race of dark skinned slaves.....: "oh how convenient."

Q: *Are the population of peoples from West Africa and the Negro's of America the same people?*

A; No. Both races of human peoples are Earth created root races, however they belong as an part to different sections of the planet Earth.. Depending on the section of Earth a human nature belongs to , the skin tone and hue will be different.

Note* Spanish explores Peter Martyr excerpt from his 1516 book De Orbe Novo.

"West Indians which are altogether in general either purple or tawny like unto sod quinces, or of the color of chestnuts or olives-which color is to them natural and not by going naked, as many have thought.. No less marvel is to consider that men are white **In Europe and Black in Africa, even with like variety are they Tawny (brown) in these Indies, with divers degrees diversely inclining more or less to black or white.** *Likewise that the men of Africa and Asia that live under the burnt line are black and not they that live beneath or on this side the same line as in Mexico, Yucatan, Quauhtema, Lian, Nicaragua, and other lands of Peru which touch the same equinoctial… It may seem that such variety of colors proceeded of man, and of Earth……although we be all born of Adam and Eve, and know not the cause why God hath ordained it.*

As noted in this 1516 excerpt the skin tone of Indigenous American people is Tawny or REDDISH Brown.

The darker skin tone and hue of the West African people is blue/purple Black -quite different.

Example: Different hue, 1. Africa (blue) 2&3 America (red)

This explains why most people can tell the difference between a person from heritage blood to Africa and a person of blood heritage to America – SIMILAR, but not the same.

The term African can apply to any dark-skinned people who look like the Earth if they are being systematically exterminated from their soil section with Earth. No populations with the planet Earth should ever accept being label Africans, whether they are from Africa or America.

Q: Well, if Indians are Dark reddish brown and Africans are blue black how did Europeans tell the difference?

A: They didn't. All people considered slaves in America

Group of Negroes to be sold as Slaves.

were captured indigenous females living in America from the Anisazi Nations of America who were captured for their Earth inheritance to their soil, Once captured renamed Negro people and deported to Jamaica, Haiti Trinidad, or other Caribbean islands, children remained on the mainland to be processes to be sold as African slaves.....

Q: Who are the people on boats in shackles shown in the images as slaves, where did they come from and where were they factually going.?

A. .The large percentage of people on the boats were females of America and their very young children. CAPTURED/ kidnapped from the interior of America for exportation in the process of de populating America of its female population, in preparation for a new immigrant population

B. *A major fact is often ignored Every inch of America was fully populated by MILLIONS of dark skinned/curly haired people of America.*

Once females and children were captured in mainland America , they became classified as (Negro's). Once they are shipped/ deported to the Caribbean, a person of America is considered separated from their Earth section inheritance to soil in America, and they are no longer considered Negro's, they are considered Africans.(or refugees as people removed or stripped from their Earth inheritance) .Once processed they are renamed as property and sent back as slaves to different settlements to have there lives used as emotional labor in the colonial building of the United States. Using the human population with America was considered a natural resource commodity, just like the trees are cut, then used for building as lumber....

Trading females and their children captured by male warriors from Americas heritage in trade was the European trick/way to

depopulate America and steal from America her right to her Earth inheritance to the soil of America in future generations, .

Excerpt's Indian Slave Trade *by Allen Gallay*

"Foreigners distinguished between Africans and Amerindians – because africans (Indians who were removed from their land by sea) would arrive in the colony as slaves for private use by free people., where as free Indians were indigenous, free and in ***possession of existing rights to land. (or Earth inheritance) "***

"By the mid-seventeenth century, the English had added another rational for their enslavement[America females] by determining that the children of a slave mother inherited her condition so the slave status passed from one generation to the next.'

Q: *How can a dark-skinned person living in America know their true blood roots?*

A; By respecting the oral story of her/his roots from her/his family elders and great -grandparents. Most people considered "black" in America today are not descendants of imported slaves, they are the last descendants of free people, who are being conditioned to see themselves as SLAVES in the United States... Children of America must stop creating confusion and invalidating their ancestry as a way to live without responsibility towards their collective life and America, by giving people who have no direct relation credibility. It is not important to know every grandparent in your family. It is important to know however, where you belong by blood of your mother/grandmothers with the planet Earth.. If they are labeled Negro they carry the blood of America.. If the only word or ancestry you can trace is Indian, grandmother who was also a Negro or just the word Negro then you are a descendant of "America " who are considered living under captivity within their Earth inheritance, being used by the United States as human chattel.. Stop the dis-respect.

Q: *Why will most people labeled "black" in America today can still identify an ancestral Indian and Negro grandparent?*

A: Not to long ago during the 1900's all people born from Indian females were automatically considered Negro, all Human Nature aka Indigenous people with the AMERICAS are stigmatized as BLACK /

NEGROES. Meaning a part of the population of human nature living with America that has ageed to support the extermination of themselves by the United States who has them living under voluntary captivity of CIVIL WAR...... in the artificial world of Patriarchy.

Q: *Why are my ancestors Indian and I am not?*

A: Whether a person identifies themselves as having Black Blood with Indian Blood, you are a last direct descendant by blood for America "Nations of Anisazi/first Indians of America, Amerindians. You a new life creation form the peoples for the planet Earth. You are the complete creation, you come from one of the oldest and are the creation of the original peoples of Earth. It does not matter what is outside of you, Take stock in the blood that YOU represent... Every mutation of our indigenous humanity to Earth wants some of the power with life possessed in our blood, while killing out the females that has the power to create the people representing America for Earth.. Over the generations of foreign manipulation and trickery used against the intellectual perceptions of the children of America from constantly conditioning the population to accept/ apply the renaming of their Earth heritage to America., the foreigners collectively as the United States, has dismembered America ancestral connection to itself, distorted America racial characteristics for heritage identity and has omitted "America" from their PUBLIC

41

education of history for the United States.

The 1st term for "OUR" Ancestors was   America, and Amerindians females) the 2nd was   American Indian,(Males) 3rd is   Negro. Now the 4th new term of trickery the United States wants us to   adopt   is African American.

*The true identity of the "blacks" in America ,
they are the Indigenous peoples creating the
human Nature of America past and present.*

*America is **OUR** continent Our home with Earth!*

✦

America & Africa

"Sister Continents for Earth,

Sister races created by Earth

but <u>different kind of peoples- belonging to two different continents."</u>

✦

Anisazi/Negro people are the Human expression of Nature for the Western Hemisphere section with the planet Earth called America's. For the last 500 years are living under an artificially created world called the United States on their home with Earth.

It's our Planet- Hosting their World!!!

43

All Negro people's Ancestral Grandmothers Heritage

AN EMBLEM OF AMERICA.

All this native land talk, (Africa)however, is nonsense.

The native land of the American Negro is America. ~ Frederick Do

Chapter 3

"America"

Artificial Identities

" The Swindle"

A Game of Influence

Q.. *What is the purpose of Artificial identity's ?*

A.   Artificial identification is a cover over something or some, in order to become invisible. This form of trickery is used in passive collective warfare against   the   human   population belonging to a section of Earth;   without, directly fighting them...

It is used to separate a indigenous   population   under political attack from their human rights to their   collective heritage   wealth – accumulated over many generations , , produced by the people using their   creativity and ingenuity in the   development for the advancement of their quality   of life ; with their section of Earth .

Artificial identities are used by foreigners as a cloak to hide what is being stolen from the collective human population under attack. Once artificial identities are accepted, these identities blindfold the people and misdirect their future generations ability to connect the crimes of theft from the past that is effecting them in the present. Distorting the future generations ability to see how to stop the attack against their collective humans conscious ability to use for their collective self esteem, self-actualization, collective self-determination, and collective self-reliance as the human nature to Earth.   Artificial identities are used to stigmatize to subjugate the population connected to the section of Earth sense of value and self respect. It is used as a way to destroy the human emotional sense of wellbeing connected to   the section of Earth, and corrupting the innate emotional natural consciousness from a sense of   equality to inferiority.

Q. How do Artificial identities work?

A.   Once a Human population or human Nature connected to a section of the planet discovered (uncovered). The foreigners as (mankind) starts exploration as trade with the new Human nature population discovered. The foreigners immediately stake claim over the human population by adopting/claiming the indigenous population names for themselves as artificial identities for themselves

Example: Alberigo Vaspuchy changed his name to Americus Vespuchy using the indigenous identity connection to reflex the claim to the new section of Earth he discovered, as the New World, and he attached/ replaced the human population for the America's identities with inferior colonial names of conquest.

. Bait & Switch

As the trade exchange grows between the indigenous population with their section of Earth and the foreigners (mankind) for inorganic products(trinkets and beads). The foreigners start influencing the young adult populations to adopt foreign attitudes of thinking, (perceptions) beliefs, and ways of living that will change the natural behavior towards their relationship with Earth . As foreign influences thru trade continues and expands . The people willing to accept the foreign influence will integrate and spread the vice (CON-artificial belief-Lie) as facts to their people and young. Once the young people start to accept themselves by the dehumanizing artificial names instead of their respectful indigenous names for expressing their humanity (collective human nature) with their inheritance section for Life with Earth.

The Quest for complete domination over the people takes hold, once the foreigner's artificial names become the main identity used between the indigenous people among themselves to reference their population living in their section of Earth. The indigenous population over time, from using the artificial identities , will result in the future generation's for a section of Earth losing their knowledge of their history for their heritage and can now be influenced(educated) to accept a new narrative connected to the artificial identity being used to cloak them....

The new narrative (history)created by the foreigners under these new artificial identities will stigmatize and dehumanize the people's heritage, while omitting the collective development of the people thru their culture as a part of the soil with Earth. The new narrative will emotionally attack the life ability of the people ; break the indigenous peoples innate conscious respect for themselves,; sense of collective unity received from the inheritance to ancestral wealth behind the indigenous/ original identities; and cloak the existence of ancestral riches stolen from their heritage culture and the theft of the ancestral wealth inheritance to the the soil, belonging to them as indigenous populations with their section of Earth.

This process of conquest is repeated for all aspects of their heritage culture for life continuation of the people with their soil.. Emotional dehumanization as attitudes of prejudice fueling self- discrimination, and individulism allows the foreigners to safely pillage/ co-opt every emotional expression of creativity belonging to the indigenous population by foreigners, until every aspect of the Natural emotional expression of the population can no longer recognize themselves and goes consciously extinct from self destruction....

.Example : Human Nature (human kind) is Hetero sexual – Male & female= ONE Life= is natural

Foreigners ideal (mankind) -is- Homo sexual- Man& man,, woman & Woman = NO LIFE- is Artificial/ extinction

Today Human Nature populations of the Earth are being influenced to accept themselves also as being homo sexual as a form of their nature. This is not true this is artificial intellectual corruption.

There is a saying '***Repeat of a Lie often enough and the Lie becomes the truth.***'

Once indigenous humans accept this intellectual corruption for themselves ,as being an artificial form of nature as homosexuals- they will stop enforcing being their natural hetero sexual aka Human expression of nature for their section of Earth.

Anytime indigenous heritage peoples intellectual perceptions accepts any forms of unnatural attitudes to use as a part of its consciousness, the collective of people who adopt these beliefs are positioned to lose the power of protection from Earths true consciousness .

Again the foreigners will stake a claim to the right of indigenous populations heterosexual natures to have natural procreation.. and replace the corrupted Human Nature with themselves as the new human beings to nature with the only right to heterosexual reproduction.... The original Human nature now corrupted will be labeled mankind to their own soil with their planet Earth.

Q: ***Who represents America today?***

A.   Unfortunately, Once the people of America allowed and accepted the settlement of immigrants to live with them on their Earth inheritance. America was changed by the foreighners to a represent their ideal for America. The symbol was changed to a European woman named "Columbia" as the new blood taking over America.

> ***In the "American Dictionary of the English Language Noah Webster 1828" the definition of American is defined as "A native of America; originally applied to the aboriginals, or copper-colored (light-dark brown skinned) races, found here by the Europeans; but now applied to the descendants of Europeans born in America. "***

Q: *What happened to the Nations of America aka Anisazi people to make them VANISH in the 1700's?*

A;   They didn't vanish at all.. . Once the new form of social culture was forcibly established against females of America by the males of America " creating the new order of the natural world" *as Patriarchy. As the establishment of patriarchy took over America females control over their life   support   inheritance   of America's soil. An allegiance was forged between   the*

50

foreigners and America Males as American Indians to form a Patriarchal government called the United States.

The Anisazi females population as "America" was given a new artificial identity of "Negro" in the new homogenous(all male) Patriarchal society. The purpose of the new identity in the new patriarchal society of men, is to separate females of America from their inheritance to wealth "from her Blood transferred to her offspring descendants who will be in receivership to the soil of America. .

Separating "America" name connection to its people would be done by the males of America supporting the establishment of patriarchy as the new way of living in America. This was done by capturing and selling the adult females to Europeans for deportation from America and selling the remaining children as slaves in America, as the way to claim their heritage inheritance, race identity, culture and to harness the knowledge used by the females of America to promote tremendous quantities of natural wealth used to nurture life in America..

 The separation process to break the blood connection awareness within the Anisazi females to their larger external selves represented in the soil, and live as people without their connection to their external life body took generations of trauma and genocide against the female and children of America population.. by the United States.

ARTIFICAL Names is a form of Trickery a Con used to hide a
theft

"*Names are like magic*

Markers in the Long

and labyrinthine streams

of racial memory

of humankind (Earthkind) is stored.

To rob people or countries

of their names is to

set in motion

a psychic disturbance

that can in turn create

a permanent crisis

of identity.

As if to underline this fact,

the theft of

an important place."

(Fulcrums of Change, Jan Carew)

Q: *Are the people TODAY called Cherokee or North and Southeastern Indians the real Indians of America?*

A: **No.** These identities are the first artificial identities created by the males of America establishing their form of social culture as Patriarchy. The patriarchal social system reversed the natural right of blood inheritance transferred to children from their mothers' blood belonging to a section of Earth - to an artificial right of males as (GOD) owners over life produced by Earth. From this reversal created an artificial inheritance from an indirect connection to blood with the people of America, This muted connection allowed the establishment for children born from unions of European females with America males as fathers to be recognized as the NEW descendants of America in the United States.

Today's Native Americans are descendants of European female settlers who were used to claim soil by having children with Men *of America.* Men of America are the foundation for the European bloodline connection to America. This ancestral connection to America thru men gives them an hybrid connection to the blood of America. They are the first artificial form of America by blood mixing as hybrids. That is why they are called

Native Americans of the United States.
The people who are considered today as the Five Civilized Tribes / Cherokee Indians or Native Americans are the descendants from the Spanish integration/ peaceful settlement into America before the official establishment of the United States.. *They are an artificial form of America and have no ancestral claim.*

Native America of the United States have chosen to adopt some of the ancestral heritage way of life conscious, culture, and traditions belonging to America aka Anisazi (Negro) people but not their fight or plight to sustain life in their home with Earth America...

Q: **Why are indigenous people of Americas in Media look Asian.**

A.   Asians are the first migrants into America. These people are called Mestizos'. The mestizos are people who are mixed with Asian and any form of American men (Indian), or Spanish /European (White) blood*. However, in the images of America Indians as men used in movies are actually Italian actors. .*

Q: *Who qualifies to be a "NATIVE AMERICAN"*
of the United State?

A: In the constitution of the UNITED STATES, a
Native American is:

1) All persons born within the jurisdiction of the
United States are considered natives.

2.) <u>Natives</u> will be classed into those <u>born before
the declaration of our independence</u> and those
born since.

All persons, without regard to the place of birth,
who were born before the declaration of
independence, <u>who were in the country at the time
it was made</u>, and who yield a deliberate assent to it,
either express or implied as remaining in the
country, are considered as *NATIVE*.

NATIVES WHO ARE <u>NOT</u> CITIZENS ARE INDIANS AND NEGROES.

Note*(In other words) anybody who was on the Anisazi soil, (America) that was under control by the Europeans at time of the declaration of independence

=

(creation of the United colonial States),and anybody born since on the **SOIL OF AMERICA** declared under the control of the United States are considered Native Americans .

Excluded are the original Peoples of America

= Indians/Negro = Black Americans today.

This means everybody or anybody that is not Indigenous aka Negro or black .

You are Anisazi People, the Natives of America not the United States......

Q: *What does the term "NATIVE AMERICAN" mean?*

A: Anyone with European blood or 3/4 European and 1/4 Indigenous (Black American / Negro) Blood

can live on Native American reservations: Southwestern (Asian/Negro) and Northwestern

(Asian/Negro/ Russian) people. However you

must be born from a immigrant female considered

a United States citizen...

56

Q: *Why aren't Negro/black Americans born from America females considered Native Americans?*

A: Because you are Indigenous or blood creation of the Earth section called America aka Negro. Children born from females of America using the health system of the United States, are automatically claimed as property(dependent) and are placed under the classification of Captive as Negro. America is being used as a possession of the United States. The sacred covenant for Earth inheritance contained in the indigenous female blood is no longer recognized. in this artificial society.

However, regardless of the make believe- the LIFE Bloodline inheritance for Earth only comes from the indigenous females to America created by Earth for the soil in America aka Anisazi/ America females, not the men. All people of black America are the real " children of America"

America the Beautiful

"The Earth children of "America" who look like the soil in America They carry the precious blood of America from the Earth. All indigenous blooded people have the love and power of life with Earth within their blood.. they are a part of life on Earth, everything else in their location, is a foreigner or a mutation of one."

It is as simple as that!!!!

Q. *How did the male population of America originally given the foreign name as American Indians change to Negro's?.*

A.   Since the 1868 civil war treaty known as the **Public Land Trust** created as a result of the American Indian males ,the original confederates or moors LOSING THE WAR for stopping the trade of human trafficking of the females population of America and children with in claimed territories being put under patriarchal governance defined as the United States.

The "Trust" was created to make the United States administrators and protectors over the Earth inheritance to the tremendous Human nature natural resources of the America belonging to America aka Anisazi females and their future generations placed behind the artificial identity of NEGRO. The artificial identity of "America" as American Indians was made trustee/Beneficiary in the trust, consisting of 770 million acres of Earth encompassing the southern portion of North America. Once accepted by the rivaling parties All American Indians as men name was removed from being free people as American Indians. Once the males of America born before 1868 died out, the new generations of males of "America" status was changed to Negro's the same as their mother status becoming dependents of the United States. The United States changed the title name for the United States into the United States of America.

The Public Trust placed all of the Earth inheritance to America now and in the future belonging to the population of people to America aka Anisazi female under United States jurisdiction. The Department of War was changed to the Department of the Interior.

Example Indians being refered to as Negro

INDIAN AND NEGRO.

From the Macon (Ga.) Telegraph, Oct. 22.

It is a travesty upon civilization that the United States has tortured into ruin the fine race that inherited the soil and has adopted a horde of African savages to educate, ride with in the cars, sit with in the theatres, and eat with white folks at the hotels. The Indian who fails to be born a negro hereafter makes the mistake of his life.

The New York Times

Published: October 28, 1886

Translation

IT IS ATRAVESTY UPON CIVILZATION THAT THE UNITED STATES {Males of America in union with European men following the directives from European men to establish the roman social culture of Patriarchy} **HAS TORTURED**{sexually abused, killed, persecuted, scalped, traumatized, to make into slaves, and deported for depopulation} **INTO RUIN**{ depopulated, domesticated, forced into a new artificial consciousness} **THE FINE RACE THAT INHERITED THE SOIL**{ America as Anisazi females} **AND HAS ADOPTED A HORDE OF AFRICAN SAVAGES-**{Anisazi males of America no longer keeping their allegiance to life with their Earth by supporting their masculine purpose as protectors for the planet Earth section as America} **TO EDUCATE-**{ Teach how to read and write}**,RIDE WITH IN THE CARS.SIT WITH IN THE THEATRES, AND EAT WITH WHITE FOLKS AT THE HOTELS.. THE INDIAN**{Anisazi male of America still living free in patriarchy }**WHO FAILS TO BE BORN A NEGRO**{ born from America/ Anisazi female living under captivity} **HEREAFTER MAKES THE MISTAKE OF HIS LIFE.**

Q: *Well, if black Americans are the "children of America", why are our people in high profile positions as leaders, politicians, clergy, and educators promoting to the children of America to see ourselves as imported people in captivity as being from Africa and to disrespect our heritage origins given to us by our parents and elder grandmothers, and forget the truth?*

A.   Unfortunately, Afro- centrism is the ideal for people who have loss respect for their heritage collective, and suffer from collective self-hate as elitist . They see themselves as superior to the people they are born from. It is used as an artificial cloak for separation, by people whom are participating in the swindle and exploitation of their kinfolk for personal gain. A way for the children of America following self-centered Patriarchal consciousness as Americans, to exploit the emotional wounds of longing resulting from the sense of lost of connection to their heritage cultural consciousness within their kinfolk without actually supporting anything to help their kinfolk. Children of America who embrace afro- centrism are not looking to put an end to foreign patriarchal supremacy, racism, poverty or oppression they are just trying to improve their position in it at the expense of their kinfolk and future children of America existence... Example; the theory of

Evolutionism, as All Negro humanity evolved out of Africa is rhetorically semantic racism.

Q: *Why didn't my grandparents tell me the whole story?*

A: Mainly because they don't know all of it. The females belonging to America were and still are being emotionally traumatized, as a result of the Patriarchal social culture system , that promotes attitudes for feminicide of them , they live in constant fear of torture from the males their blood created, they don't know all the details to why the covert war they are living to survive thru is against them and the natural consciousness for life in them is often times oppressed and severely compromised. Their life stories are filled with memories of surviving through living with many forms of emotional violation, emotional trauma ,pain, all forms of physical & sexual abuse , neglect and fear against their gender..

"OUR" Ancestral grandmothers " America", like today had to learn how to become invisible to their Ancestral culture consciousness, silent about their heritage and survive form the dehumanizing treatment of being rape, sexually tortured, and used for Slaves, to co- exist in an artificial world being developed by foreign MEN on their section

63

of the planet Earth in order to survive, in the only soil they knew. Yesterday is like today, Millions of families belonging to America are constantly being broken up by institutionalized foreign intervention. Not too long ago, most children of America were taken from their mothers by the time they were 5 to 7 years old. Oral history was given while they were young so they would not forget who they were, and one day figure out why there is a war being waged against them. As a result from emotional trauma over many generations, many children of America as elders only remembered that they had "Indian Blood."

Q: Why do people label black "America" today dismiss their Indian Ancestral identity?

A: Since the development of television, the United States entertainment industry has used Italian immigrants to the United States to play the role of American Indian males in movies. This is another European Distortion of the truth. However there is NO representation of "America' females promoted in her natural glory in the United States.

"America is Negro"

The important undeniable visual fact about .America aka Anisazi females are light to dark skinned and have textured hair not straight hair and the real heritage for "America" is the Negro females. has been kept secret and invisible by the society at large. Many children of America as Negro's dismissed the precious gift of knowledge about who they are, because of the promoted distorted images of America in the United States is different than their mothers skin color and hair that represents America.

Instead the females for "America" heritage are stigmatized in the society as not included in the society. They should be regarded as inferior, untrustworthy, ignorant, ugly, as human animals, to be used like captured animals as powerless slaves ……so any story about them will do…. The fact the identity of Negro, represent the Earth children of America is ignored…

The secret truth is the continents of the western hemisphere as America is the Garden of Eden on Earth given to America aka Negro females for her children to be fruitful and multiply. This is the reason why over the last 500 years in America children born from America's females are persecuted from discrimination, imprisonment,, stigmatized and oppressed, living in poverty, under the occupation(police and law) of the United States and other Colonial governments with the support of America's elite or 1%

"Our kids, America's children, so often are isolated, without hope, less likely to graduate from high school, less likely to earn a college degree, less likely to be employed, less likely to have health insurance, less likely to own a home. A part of this is a legacy of hundreds of years of slavery and segregation and structural inequalities that compounded over generations. "

President Barack Obama, NAACP Annual Convention 2015

The fact: All foreigners collectively are at war with all people created to live with Earth ,born from females portals for Earth is an global issue, and the war against the children of America in the Western hemisphere is just another component of the planetary extermination of the human consciousness connected to the planet Earth..

The political agenda used against the children of America in the United States is an ongoing and are massive social campaigns of ethnic cleansing through social influences targeted to isolate the human consciousness of the females expression towards sustaining life of their people and corrupting the natural consciousness of the females and males of America for unity . Today millions of males are completely disconnected from their kind of females species and America females are disconnected from the feminine expression of themselves, if not corrected will lead the remaining children of America into their self-extermination out of their planetary Earth inheritance to the soil of America,. Stopping the influence from artificial perceptions is at the core of the problem. However, there is a catch, the human nature of "America" is a vital part of the life force for America, with Earth, without the combination of the children of America and the vitality of the environment of America that supports life in America. Human Life and nature as we know it will cease to exist,

The United States may write America out of their History, however the children of America will never forget America is our LIFE LINE home with Earth.

Q. *Why is keeping the record straight about our heritage important?*

A. THE UNITED STATES WILL WRITE THE EXISTENCE OF THE HUMAN NATURE POPULATION OF "AMERICA" OUT OF THEIR HISTORY?

In 1705 the America's was split and the males of America separated themselves from the females who create them. America as a collective name for the female blood connection to her soil was changed to Negro, and according to the United States education dogma, 1700's is the time the ancestral heritage of America as a whole , (with America males and females in unity) identified as the Mississippian culture and their continental civilization called the Moundbuildres of America mysteriously vanish, of course leaving tremendous amount of produced riches and wealth for the newly created all male patriarchal social system taking over America as the United States to pillage and claim as their own.. Over the last 3 generations the heritage of America as the Negro People are being influenced to adopt another artificial foreign identity of African Americans, the Negro race of people belonging to America will vanish from American history by 2040 as an extinct race of people who once occupied America and all the contributions to the development in the United States and accumulated wealth as Negro America will vanish and be assimilated into United States education as contributions from the heritage belonging to foreigners . The complete Negro heritage legacy will be robbed /stolen from the children of America future generation just like the American Indian heritage legacy was stolen from them as Negro's. The future generations of America now invisible will be positioned to be considered as immigrant slaves to the only soul and soil their ancestors ever knew..

Q. *Why is it important for all children of America as Negro's blacks to never forget their ancestral legacy as America?*

A. 1 .Collectively We are America-we are the human nature stewards and trustee's for the soil with Earth the United States wants to call home.

2. The United States is not America. United States is using/ occupying/killing America.

3 All Negro people in the US are in fact the first citizens of the United States from their grandfathers investment of forcing the females of America to share their inheritance with the newly created United States..

4. The children of America ancestral grandfathers allowed the Earth of America heritage **to** be used for the creation & development of   the United States.

5.Since 1868 the United States creation of the Public Land Trust for the American Indian heritage land.. as trust administrators the United States must make sure Americas and her children can flourish on their section of Earth.

6. The children of America as Negro can keep pressure to hold the   United States accountable for trying to rob them of their Earth inheritance and the United   States obligation to stop racism against them as its original citizens....

Q. *What will happen if the children of America as Negro, allow   the United States to change their name into   another artificial identity   meaning immigrants from Africa?*

A.   A. The price to life paid:, the Population belonging to America can be erased from historical existence with America as   HISTORICAL   ETHNIC   CLEANSING.   The population has always been seen as socially unwanted. Now under the stigma of refugee. The United States can remove their naturalization of citizenship for them making them non-naturalized immigrants to the United States, therefore creating a way for them to be excluded as being a part of the United States or America- leading to COMPLETE MARGINILIZATION   AND   DEPORTATION   from the United States in America. The new generations of children of America as African Americans can be completely severed from all human and fundamental indigenous rights inherited to them from their planet Earth to America. The people of America, at one time labeled as the

Negro population will again artificially vanish from America in the United States along with the entitlements gained from their civil rights treaty with the United States in 1968. Just like their ancestors of America before them labeled AMERICAN INDIAN artificially vanished, along with the treaties and agreements made with our Anisazi ancestors as American Indians to share living in America as a patriarchal country governed by foreign and America males after 1775,, and the erasing of their heritage civilization and culture with the population of America in their original identity of Anisazi ,the planet keepers who lived in America since the beginning of Earth time; once they adopted their new Ethnic placement under the artificial identity of NEGRO

B. The Public Land Trust of 770 million acres of soil with America that belongs to the current children of America, the United States claims to be administrators over ,will no longer have trustee's of the Amerindian race of people aka American Indians and Negros, because they have abandoned their own heritage Life consciousness with there soil., therefore America has vacated or died out of her Earth trust. The United States can legally and civilly as administrators claim the Earth Inheritance to America as their own, . Under the artificial identity as foreigners to America the future generations of America's children can be influenced to vacate their home with Earth rights and be forced to immigrate to a foreign section of Earth and legally be deported by the United States from their home with Earth without lifting a gun.

Genocide Complete.

Q, W*hat happens if we do accept a new artificial name and foreign narrative of ancestral heritage for our people and future generations?*

A   . Under this new artificial identity of African   American, the children of   America will be   robbed again, lose their fundamental, political, and international   rights recognition to have a their place to belong with Earth'

THE   FUTURE   GENERATIONS   OF   THE CHILDREN   OF   AMERICIA   WILL   BE REDUCED   TO   THE   MOST   INFERIOR PEOPLE on Earth .

The consequences from the negligence of the elders   of   America today, for allowing the United States to classify their future generations for the heritage (blood) for America AS   IMMERGRANT refugees, from somewhere other than America.

The future population of America will lose their   political ability to stop the United States from removing their right to live with America in the United States. The future generations will become a disposed people.

We Don't have to be Victims by following the mistakes of the past.

It is time to Learn from the mistakes of the past....

"United States as a country has reneged on all its commitments and signed agreements with America's patriarchy and is refusing to abide by international law in policy towards them. Then turns around, and blames the children of America who are its victims for all the poverty, discrimination, and violence against them, while holding the whole nation of America captive and at the same time blaming its victim for its own belligerence and its own destructive policies towards them."

Our conscious Evolution is our Revolution....

Conclusion

Why do black "America" lives matter?

The United States have a forgotten partner in its development as a country. It is a forgotten fact the United States was created by two different races of males for the establishment of Patriarchy, as the new social culture on the soil of America. The United States is a partnership between the warriors of America and the European males as traders, without Americas warriors(grandfathers) approval to peaceful settlement and sharing of the soil inheritance belonging to the females of America (grandmothers) as Negro. There would not be a United States today..... this is one of the most important facts all black America should never forget today...

For generations, millions of America children have found ways to participate in the new patriarchal society as the United States, and abandon their responsibility to the future generations of America to live free with their Earth inheritance, however, the United States as a patriarchal imperial government of foreign (European) males have never accepted the people of America (Male or Female) who adopted them on their soil as equal stakeholders in the development of United States using their soil . Regardless of how they change their name, the children of America will never be a thriving part of the United States . .

People who ignore the truth will soon forget the truth and surely will be destroyed as a result of it .... RaDine America

74

Over the last 500 years of lies , cover-ups of the many crimes against the humanity to the people of America and her children for their inheritance soil, by the people of America supporting the patriarchal system of the United States has crippled the children of America into living in a perpetual state of war against their own lives.

Over generations, billions of people of Americas have wasted their lives by following unnatural perceptions of the American Dream with its hedonistic believe systems of death as the purpose of life with Earth, and from indulging in systems of emotional death, as selfishness, elitism, sexual exploitation, homosexualism, and individualism, for the pursuit of artificial intellectual perceptions, physical & material comfort, and entertainment that has lead the children of America, who once was a intellectually superior and strong emotional life consciousness with Earth, in to living in a state of intellectually inferior and weak life conscious development, poverty, emotional weakness, addiction, narcissism and fear..... This is the dilemma all Negro people face today as a result of following the unconscious's ways of the fairly recent past.

"The New Egyptians"

The peoples of America by adopting a new artificial identity will not help save their lives, just help seal their future in more poverty, and create more pain and suffering in life as they move towards their collective extinction.

Today is no different from yesterday, the United States is still influencing ' the children of America into believing and practicing in the artificial homosexual consciousness of mankind instead of keeping the human Nature heterosexual consciousness of their planet Earth, and are still determined to erase the FUTURE GENERATIONS from the females who carry the blood from Earth to America ... Unfortunately, today all indigenous people of the Western hemisphere are at the same crossroads of life or death..

Ignorance of these simple facts is at the core of the problem young America finds themselves grappling with today. The truth is;

All people labeled "Negro in the America's" are the last of the ancient bloodlines of the feminine expression of Earth for the America's.. They are the Children of Earth., and carry the power of Earth consciousness in their blood. It is time for transformation of consciousness.

If they learn from the mistakes from the past. They do not have to pay the consequences of doom left for them by the misguided generations before them.

Revealing the larger Picture- "The Laws of Earth"

It is time to acknowledge some simple yet powerful Truths:

1. The people of America created by the planet Earth to live with the soil of America are innately nurturing, emotionally gentle, kind and loving people.

2. The females and their children of America are still persecuted from artificial illusion, life violated and killed with impunity in the United States, by the United States systematic efforts to remove them from their inheritance to America for the last 500 years.

3. Yet, America's people have caused no harm to life on Earth and have started no wars against any other people on Earth.

4. America's people, have not stolen or killed any peoples children or brought to any people any form of disease...

5. The females of America have not mutated her blood with other people, nor have we converted any males to go against the laws of nature.

6. We have uplifted the life support of other people all over the Earth from using our life technologies. from our culture

7. We have not wandered off to become immigrants from our section of Earth to break the laws of the Earth and corrupt another part of nature with the Earth.

We the Earth children with America are surviving thru collective persecution and are forced to watch the corruption of Earth consciousness into the unnatural consciousness of MAN, that is destroying out life support system living with America. For generations, We have watched foreign people come to our body of Earth, stake claim to our Earth, culture, identity, and rob the future life of our children.

"There is another hidden and forgotten truth"

Life of Earth loves us too........

The children of America has lived with their Earth since the beginning of Earth time. The laws that govern Life of Earth are in full effect and has recorded all the actions taken towards the distortion and destruction of the inner sense of life, of it laws and consciousness for the life expression of Earth.

All wrongs done to life of Earth including human will be rectified by Earth. The law of life of Earth will not allow itself to be robbed of its people in its image and reflection. The planet Earth will never live without its own expressions of creation as some form of mixed mutation. If the children of Earth as America do not thrive in their body America, nothing will be able to live on America.

" All children of America lives Matter"

It is time the children of America's heritage take stock in the gift of Life heritage to America from their mothers, and respect the value of the blood in their veins, stop ignoring their Life heritage to Earth. and learn about the emotional consciousness living in their blood so they will know how to work with the Earth power within them to transform an evolve themselves, and heal our planet..

Our revolution from the fate of extinction is our evolution from the intellectual unconsciousness of mankind to our human consciousness with Earth.

We as the human part of "America" nature, as children of the Life heritage blood for America has a responsibility to stand for the life of our blood as America and keep secure the life blood of America for the future of our life with Earth inheritance. We must never forget our true heritage and to stand against the lies from the United States that is tricking the people for America into their own self destruction.

"Another World is Possible," emerged out of a completely new mentality, when people recognized that essentially those in control are dysfunctional and that the old social democracy dependence on those in power to give you things, that period is over."

The late "Grace Lee Boggs"

"All of us are beneficiaries of a strong black (America) woman."

President Barack Obama   Congressional Black Caucasus   speech 2015

79

Could this be Little Richards Great, Great Grandfather????

Looks like Little Richard

The Prophet

The Prophet promised the people they would be immune to the white man's tricks, if they would only return to the old ways.

Picture: George Catlin , North American Indians

What did the children of America share to be a part of the United States?

AMERICA.

The biggest contribution black America grandfathers as American Indians shared for the creation of the United States is our home on Earth inheritance belonging to the blood of their grandmothers.

"America"

William Katz, author of the book <u>Black Indians</u> comments on racial distortion, (page 17):

> *"Distorting racial history, as teachers know, injures Dark Children. They live with muted heritage. Despite Black Indians' contributions to their land, neither Negro, nor Indian children, nor the current adult population have awareness of this Legacy."*

> *"LIKE WHITES, Native Americans learned in school that Africans were contented slaves and had no fighting traditions; certainly none that allied them with the Indians. For their part, Afro-Americans are aware of Indians in their family tree but probably assume that like the whites (a further distortion) lurking there, they are mere intruders. Such inaccurate beliefs hide a heritage worth exploring further; dividing people today that could truly benefit from unity.*

'However, this book also maintains the distortion of racial identity. The racial identity of the Indian remains invisible. This omission of racial identity allows the reader to believe the Indians and the Africans were two different races of people distinguished by skin color, and who, by chance, mixed with each other. Of course, the African blood "washed out" the Indian Blood. That's why you have Black Indians when, in fact, they were the same. They were Negro people termed Indians from North America Nation of Mound Builders, fighting for their freedom to live and not be enslaved

..Even William Katz does not want to tell *that* part of the truth!

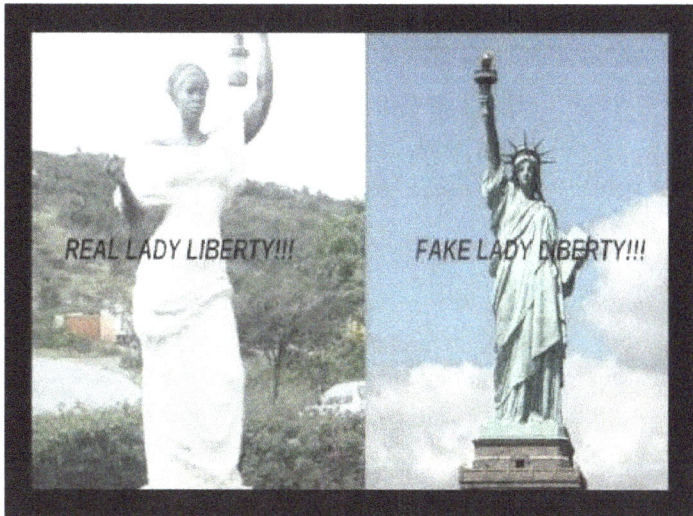

Secret Identity of the Statue of Liberty

The story of Lady Liberty is one that all children of America people can be proud of. It is a gift given to "America" people to represent the power of there heart.

The evolution of this central icon in the American Identity is the focus of Faces of A Nation at the Long island Museum of American Art, History & Carriages. 2001

It is written:

" **Lady Liberty has undergone several transformations in identity, and style. Long before we had the Statue of Liberty in New York Harbor, The Indian Princess symbolized the New World. Over time the Indian Princess became less "native" and more European. Her skin grew lighter, her features became less "Indian" and her dress was adapted to the mode of the moment."**

The Statute of Liberty represented the power of freedom and human consciousness over oppression.

The English/Germans after winning the French War in America, expelled the French for the control of the industry, wealth, culture and lands belonging to Indian Heritage(females) in America. The civil war was not a war over slavery as much as it was a war between the Indians and European immigrants. . The Anisazi People, now termed Indians, were fighting to preserve their heritage rights of self determination and freedom on their Earth against the European influence of Patriarchy, capitalism, extortion, exploitation, and oppression. After the Indians won the civil war a treaty was adopted to create a union between the two peoples in the land of America establishing the United States of America The French sent the Black skinned, wide hips and feathers as her head crown lady, as a reminder to the United States of who actually won the war that is called the Civil war. The United States changed the symbol to erase the Black American peoples memory of the power with-in the conscious resolve of their ancestral Indian grandmothers heritage that created the Garden of Eden called America. Today the power of Lady Liberty is still distorted by Black American historians (African Americans) who prefer to maintain her invisibility to her people an identify her as a African woman instead of dealing with the truth of who she represents as the Ancestral Indian Grandmother heritage belonging to the Anisazi people now termed Black Americans. The truth about Lady Liberty would empower the Black American people with the knowledge to reclaim their stolen heritage, history and legacy in America. Lady Liberty is a statue to show tribute to all the Black American people power of their Indian Grandmothers conscious resolve for the future generations to keep their Earth free from oppression..

The Solution-

Stop supporting your Ethnic cleansing from America

Children of America

have a choice

Just say NO

To artificial identities

To unnatural ways of life consciousness

Stop supporting crimes against your humanity

To praying for death and to the dead

*Stop supporting the killing of our children's future
and America.*

Just say YES!!!!

To life-Lift your voices in truth

We are America not Americans

*Pray for LIFE with Earth and the strength to fulfill
your purpose to Life*

*To evolving from the mistakes of the past in creating
a future for life on Earth.*

All children of the western hemispheres called Negros

Stand in your human right from Nature

85

Stand with Life – stand in TRUTH

We are America

We are not immigrants. We have a right to Live......

Support the petition

We Are America

America lives Matter!!!!!

If you are a Negro or descendant of Negro parentage and ancestry, you qualify to be recognized for your human right to ethnic identity classification . if you want to be recognized for your human rights and indigenous rights to America sign the

We are America Petition
http://www.ipetitions.com/petition/we-are-america

What can I do?

1 - Read documentation and sign the petition online at http://fiaah.org/community-voices/petitions .

2 - . Learn about *Foundation for Indigenous Americans of Anisazi Heritage /www.fiaah.org*

if you have Negro/ American Indian Heritage(ancestral grandmothers etc)   You can register with the America Heritage Registry be to recognize and learn how to be a part of indigenous America, you can get an America Heritage Registry application@.

http://fiaah.org/departments/department-of-america-heritage If you qualify. Fill out and Sign

3.Tell someone about the book and share the knowledge. 4.Ask your elders   over 70 to tell you   their   true stories.... And listen!!!!!

5. Collect their race identification papers make copies....

5. Learn and raise your consciousness *The Institute for Indigenous America Studies* is a private educational institute for people indigenous to America who are registered with the America Heritage Registry. The Institute provides continuation of development in traditional, Earth consciousness and heritage technology .
www.indigenousamericastudies.institute

✦

American Indians, Negroes,
Are todays black America
Descendants of the Anisazi Nations of
"America"
the original Earth- Pyramid/Mound builders
have NOT been abandoned
by the Holy Spirit of Earth...
they are NOT cursed by Life!
When United in consciousness
Manifest
the Greatest Healing Power
for life of Earth!

✦

Index of Questions

Chapter 3 – Artificial Identities The "Game" of Influence

About the Author

"There are few instances in our lives when we meet a person who is truly Divine.

Rev. RaDine is one such person" Antionio Green- Rolling Out Magazine

Ambassador RaDine America Harrison is a proud full blooded female of America , born from the Anisazi heritage linage union of Chickasaw mother and Cherokee/Aniyumwija/ father. She is the international representative for Anisazi aka Negro people with the Foundation for Indigenous Americans of Anisazi Heritage (F.I.A.A.H.) and the Administrative Director for the Institute for Indigenous American Studies.

As Ambassador her mission is to advocate for recognition of the children of America in the United States and all sections of America in the western hemisphere aka Negro people in international legislation to ensure protections of America indigenous People's inherited fundamental and human rights for sustaining the viability of their populations , still living in the western hemisphere in their Home on Earth as America.

She is one of the founding members of the Foundation of Indigenous Americans of Anisazi Heritage (F.I.A.A.H.) The mission of F.I.A.A.H is to assist the children of America aka people of black America to stop the racism used against them for the acquisition of their indigenous birth-right inheritance of America, heal from the emotional bondage of stigmatization and disfranchisement applied against them; and the rape of the collective wealth from there ,heritage, culture, and natural resources from their home on Earth inheritance. .

As Administrative Director for the Institute for Indigenous American Studies. Amb. RaDine A. Harrison is considered a scholar on global Indigenous issues, Indigenous America culture, traditional knowledge, heritage and history of America. She is an author of many books on "America" Negro heritage, culture and stolen legacy in the Americas.

The black American handbook for survival thru the 21st Century vol 1 is the first book published and cataloged in the United States on Negro Heritage, revealing imperial research on the origins of the ancestry for the American Negro, correcting the racism as Amnesia in U.S historical narrative for the peoples of "America" People aka Negro promoted by the institutionalized Education systems and media in the United States

Ambassador / Rev.. RaDine America Harrison ND. LMT. is also an ordained inter faith theologian, , with over 20 years' experience in traditional indigenous healing remedies, indigenous Life consciousness, ancestral culture and heritage traditions of America.............

Amb. RaDine America Harrison was asked by many to teach her wonderful awareness of life with Earth. and life consciousness understanding..

Sister RaDine America Harrison - a survivor of a near death tragedy and the loss of her first born son, during recovery was lead to uncover the larger more profound understanding about life. Surrendering control over her life to the inner consciousness of her blood, she in return received gifts beyond her wildest dreams and expectations. The most profound gift was the revealing and validation of her true heritage identity , purpose and the Ancestral identity of 150 million or more people who are being forced to live under the artificial classification of Negro and now Afro-Americans. This profound Grace alone has made it clear to her why her life and all the Ancient ones of the Anisazi/ Negro -People of America humanity is SO IMPORTANT as a part of Nature with our planet Earth. She joyfully accepts the life service for the healing of her people, which will allow the healing of all the people for Earth to return to serving their purpose to save the planet Earth…..

It is Time……. It is Time…. Time has come……… for your light…….. Look towards the sun the children of Amerriqui…………

For this dawn will bring a new day……..

For a complete overview of facts about the omitted Negro heritage and the true dynamics that is at the core foundation between the United States and it's relation to the destiny of the Indigenous population to America aka Anisazi descendants called Negro/ black Americans today.

Books authored by Ambassador RaDine America Harrison or Rev.RaDine Amen-ra

The black American Handbook- vol. I

The Forgotten Truth Behind Racism in America edition 2

$29.95   ISBN 978-0-9705455-0-3

The black American handbook for the survival through the 21ˢᵗ Century vol.2

The Book of Heritage

Ancestral Heritage& Cultural Civilization Legacy of the Negro

Getting out of the system-ebook

The Anisazi Story-ebook

The importance of Ethnic Identity-DVD

Soon to be released:

Vol. 3 the Understanding of Slavery- The capturing of America

Vol. 4 The creation of the American Negro- the colonization and assimilation of the American Indians in the United States

Order on-line www.fiaah.org

For more info contact1-877-571-9788

To do in-depth study in Americas heritage and history The Institute for Indigenous America Studies is a private institution for learning the traditional cultural knowledge of America.

For more information and enrollment about the Institute for Indigenous America Studies, go to

www. indigenousameriastudies.institute

America is like a morning glory lost in a tangle of Vines..........

Hidden in Lies but not Forgotten

Forgotten but not gone!!!

.